Una clase

por Beatrice Reynolds

Scott Foresman
is an imprint of

PEARSON

Glenview, Illinois • Boston, Massachusetts • Chandler, Arizona
Upper Saddle River, New Jersey

Every effort has been made to secure permission and provide appropriate credit for photographic material. The publisher deeply regrets any omission and pledges to correct errors called to its attention in subsequent editions.

Unless otherwise acknowledged, all photographs are the property of Pearson.

Photo locations denoted as follows: Top (T), Center (C), Bottom (B), Left (L), Right (R), Background (Bkgd)

Opener Getty Images; 1 Rubberball Productions; 3 Getty Images; 4 (B) DK Images; Getty Images; 5 (CR) © Comstock Inc.; 6 (CR) © DK Images, 6 (TL) © Dorling Kindersley; 6 (B) DK Images; 7 DK Images; 8 Rubberball Productions; 8 (B) Corbis

ISBN 13: 978-0-328-53303-9
ISBN 10:   0-328-53303-3

Copyright © by Pearson Education, Inc., or its affiliates. All rights reserved. Printed in the United States of America. This publication is protected by copyright, and permission should be obtained from the publisher prior to any prohibited reproduction, storage in a retrieval system, or transmission in any form or by any means, electronic, mechanical, photocopying, recording, or likewise. For information regarding permissions, write to Pearson Curriculum Rights & Permissions, One Lake Street, Upper Saddle River, New Jersey 07458.

Pearson® is a trademark, in the U.S. and/or other countries, of Pearson plc or its affiliates.

Scott Foresman® is a trademark, in the U.S. and/or other countries, of Pearson Education, Inc., or its affiliates.

1 2 3 4 5 6 7 8 9 10 V0G1 18 17 16 15 14 13 12 11 10 09

Mira a estos niños.
¿Qué puede ser este lugar?
¡Una clase!

La clase trabaja en equipo.
Comparten los lápices.
Dibujan en el papel.

Todos en la clase tienen tareas.

Hay un pajarito en una jaula.

Le dan agua y comida.

La clase mira fotos.

Dicen el nombre de cada animal.

Son: caballo, chancho o cerdo, pato.

A la clase le gusta jugar.

Los niños suben por detrás.

Luego se tiran por el tobogán.

Los niños toman su lugar en el autobús.
"Voy para mi casa", dice cada niño.
¿Vas tú a una clase como ésta?